HEADSPACE

Fin Hall

Janine Rae

Arya Rae

Often my daughter and I would go walking around the countryside and beaches near where we stay in the North East of Scotland.

We would talk on all things, often returning to our common interest, poetry. Although to date, she has only once been able to standup and read in public, and that was our collaborative piece. A couple of her pieces have been published in the Joined Up Writing collaboration.

Meanwhile her teenage daughter, is slowly developing her way through writing. She too has had one piece in the Joined Up Writing series.

I therefore proudly present this unique collection of poems from three generations.

To keep it in the family, the cover design was done by the talented Mark Elrick, my second cousin.

FLUX was originally published in Steel Jackdaw magazine.

LOVE was originally published in Joined Up Writing: 100 Voices under the name Adrian Rae.

Published by Like A Blot From The Blue 2023.

FATHER, GRANDFATHER.

Loss and Hope

One line to take away the grief and pain
One line just to get me through the day
One line to help me forget
One line to hide my loss and regrets.
Today, no more lines in my view
I'm learning to live each day without you
The future, if not bright,
Has hints of shine and light.

STITCH

Some days it's hard to face the reality that the world goes on outside your door,
While you struggle to get out of bed and stumble, fumble to the kitchen and pour yourself a cup of ambition.
The contrition in your head and the condition that led to the place you are now, where indecision is first choice and the small voice inside you head gets louder.
The recurring thought prevails that you are stuck between going off or staying on the rails just waiting to see what train comes first.
Another day, another dollar, the silence becomes a holler, uncertainty and confusion, is your life just an illusion?
Getting hard to sort out truth from fact.
Ambiguous and failing, you watch as the last ship is sailing, leaving the safety of the harbour:
leaving you behind.
Your mind in constant turmoil hardly knowing what is up, always feeling lowly, feeling down.
No matter how you attempt to alter, your attitude still falters, causing oscillation and dilemma,
hoping the line is not already crossed
It's ok to not be ok, it's ok to seek out help.
There are those who will offer you a hand.
Be aware that all is not lost, you don't have to pay the cost,
there are ways to help you to get through.
So when all is said and done, you know you're not alone.
There are people out there who care

I WISH

I wish I didn't love you
It would be so much easier for me
I wish you were a bad person
Instead of a caring one
I wish that you didn't have a bath run for me when I get home,
And that, sometimes, you had food ready for me to eat.
I wish I didn't hear from you daily,
Making me realise that I still love you.
I love you, but I don't like you,
And I wish you knew that there is a difference between these things
I wish my heart didn't ache every time you text me
And I wish our children didn't have to see us both suffer.
See us torn apart
Hearts broken
Where once they were open and proud
Now the silence is loud
Where two is a crowd
The house is strange,
And although you want to change,
It must come naturally
And not forced, coerced
Put on
Made.
Time alone may heal the wounds.
I wish there was another way.
I wish these yesterdays were not the way they were
As I wish you knew those days
Were days when the hurt began
Prolonged, burned deep into my heart
And, I wish I had an answer to it all.
I wish we didn't have to cry
Each day
To find a way to heal.
We have to fake it to make it through every hour,
And although I have no wish to sour things between us,
They may be irretrievable
Unable to be fixed.
Even though I wish they could.
I wish I didn't love you so much.

I WISH

I wish I could fix the hurt you feel just now
I wish, that when I hold you in my arms
the tears and pain would vanish,
I wish that I could wet my hanky and wipe off the sadness within
Or stick a plaster over the unseen scars
I wish the love I have for you would be enough to help you fall asleep
And not cry yourself to sleep.
Or read you a story and tell you it will be alright in the morning
That things will be fine after some hot milk and a biscuit.
We know that it won't be,
But I wish it was

I wish that all that there were to concern you was falling over on the way to the bus stop
And missing an appointment because we had to go home and change your clothes.
Or got lost, when you were just the other side of the shop counter

I never want to wish my life away
Nor nostalgically look back on sunny days
I just wish that I could do one of my stupid magic tricks
And make the pain disappear.
But wising doesn't help you, as you wish the same for yours.
Sharing grief
Is no relief
But making wishes with hugs and kisses,
Is all that I can do.

NOTHING SPEAKS LOUDER THAN SILENCE

Alone in the room.
The room in the house,
the empty house,
The house where voices of children were heard.
Footsteps on the stairs.
Memories of the cries of " stop running. Stop that thumping." Only echos now.
The house where music came from different teenage rooms.
The chatter land nattering of giggly voices,
going on and on about nothing.
The hammering of shelves being put up.
The clattering of dishes being loaded into the washer.
The slamming of doors.
"Stop slamming the door!"
Chopping vegetables in the kitchen.
Boiling kettles.
Crushing herbs.
Sharpening knives.
Now, a meal for one. A bed for one.
Silence is all
And there is nothing louder than silence.

LABELS

You wear your label like a badge of honour
But it disguises what you are
A human being

Like a cloud atop a mountain
A toupe made of weather,
Hiding what is beneath
A sheath
A cover

Although it's better to be woke
Than asleep
It's always better to be waking
Which means being aware of changes
Strange as things at times may seem
Life is not a dream

Labels put you in boxes
Labels make it easy for the ignorant,
For the wilful
For the cruel
To see the cracks in the labelled
Enabling them to chip away at the weaknesses
Pull apart the strengths they do not have.
Slowly, or not so slowly, bruising.
Choosing silence as a solution
Seeking absolution for the label *they* chose to wear
I care, we care,
But be aware
Of those who may chose to belittle you
Because of the label they see.

So stop using labels,
' I am, they are, ' and more
It's just a means of closing the door,
An excuse to refuse to let them be,
A part of things

Europeans only
Asians only
Americans only

Boys only
Girls only
Gays only
Trans only
Blacks only
Whites only
Men only
Women only
Christians only
Muslims only
Atheists only
Married only
Single…
We
All
Should
Just

Mingle

DANCE WHILE YOUR LIGHTS ARE LIT DARKNESS COMES TOO SOON

You need a dialogue with fear
To help you keep your ship on an even keel
Help you steer around the rocks,
Whilst,
Not being afraid of the rocks.
Be aware of the rocks,
The rocks don't know that you are there ,
You, however, know they exist.

Not everything is black and white.
But, also it's not all psychedelic colours
Not everyone is out to get you
Neither does the world owe you a sandwich
You have to make your own sandwich
But
If some one offers you salad for your sandwich
Then,

They might just be offering you salad for your sandwich.
And not wanting anything in return,
Except a simple "Thank you."

With age, they say, comes experience
But experience doesn't come with sitting at home
Sitting still, both physically and mentally
Sitting alone, prone to, well nothing.
And nothing is more than a state of mind
Nothing is a state of being
And being afraid of nothing
Is nothing short of odd
And just as complex as being afraid of everything

Sadness doesn't always howl
Sometimes it is the whispering voice at the end of the day
In your head
Asking , "Is there room in your head for one more?"

BEHIND THOSE EYES

Your needs are simple,
Comfort, a home to come back to
He doesn't worry if his dinner is not on the table
And he will deal with the baby.
Deal with whatever needs to be dealt with.
He will smile,
chat,
Be there for you,
And know who will be there for him
To get the light out from behind his eyes.

He looks at you and you are aware
That, when he says , "I'm fine."
He isn't really.
He knows you know,

But words are hard to disclose
Breathe out, and release into the void that is the world.
So inside they stay,
Day after day.
Wishing for stability.
Hoping for, just once,
To have respite from what goes on behind his eyes.

His needs are few,
Stability, normal days,
Consideration,
Situation regular.
No lofty ambitions,
He is just a white picket fence type guy,
Who has too many tears to cry.
Those who know him well, know why.

And what resides behind those eyes.

MIRROR

I wish it was before again
Before the the pain within took over
Before I stopped knowing what I know.
Before the turmoil and confusion
When I knew the difference between reality and illusion
And confidence ...
Yeah confidence,
I remember how that felt,
Not caring if I was liked,
Doing what I do,
Pretty happy, seldom blue,
Different times different mindset
Was it really, really me?

I awoke one sunny morning, or late afternoon. I can't recall
A strange sensation overcame me,
For no reason,

None at all
Couldn't put my finger on the feeling in my head
Maybe it was a bad dream, but why did it stick around?
Since then I feel, well , I'm not sure what,
Uncertainty, undermines my underpinning thoughts of hope
Confidence has left me, surely just this once.
A chance to string some words together
Pegged like washing on a rope.

Silence
Still and silent
Except for background screams within my head
Within the place where clarity once ruled
Now jumbled up
Tumbled up
Mumbled, rumbled, bumbled up
Creeping, seeping liquid thoughts,
It's brought me to this place.

This place, where I used to know
Where I used to be able to see clarity.
Where everything was alright with me
Now...

What do you see when you look in the mirror?
Do you see the normal looking
Normal feeling person that the world sees?
Or do you see a curled up, hesitant , silent screaming you?
A vision of confidence ,
Or a vision of incertitude?
Flapping in the summer breeze where thoughts and dreams blow away.
Where no one sees the pain within,
Turning cold in a sudden whim.

A broken arm or another limb
Gets fixed and signed by friends and others
But a broken mind then no one bothers.
They keep their distance as there is no autograph to give
upon a troubled mind.

ONLY TIME CAN BREAK YOUR HEART

It's been 52 years since I first heard After The Gold Rush.
52 years.
52 years before that it was the end of the First World War.
52 years.
At the same time, same place, I heard When I'm Dead And Gone.
52 years later I'm still here.
Back then it would have been still a few years to go before my daughter was even thought of.
Doesn't that make you stop and think?
To wonder, to ponder,
Where times goes?

FLUX

Somewhere in my past
Is a future waiting to be found
The sound of memories, some broken
Are littered on the ground.
My head recoils at thoughts unkind
A life that happened whether you want it or not.
The spot that never heals
Conceals many flaws
And laws that you never knew existed.
Watch out, it will have caught up with you.
Taken you unawares
As you stared into the abyss
Trying to see what you might become
Long past scared,
Crimes with rhymes from times still to be
Awaken the dead
Who are yet to be born
Forlorn hopes and dreams that in the future you had
Erasing time before it gets here
But the truth is, that there is no journey.
We are all arriving and departing at the same time.

If you think
Therefore you will be
As you are, before,
as the door to the past
Is the portal to the future where
Sutures help to seal the wound
But some time alone heals them.
You can scheme and plan and try to escape
The best is yet to come
Even Ornette Coleman knew, or he will know
That tomorrow is the question
Answer when you can,
If you haven't already.

Time is flux, it breathes in many places
Checking you out as you check in.
It will play with you
Toy with you
All the while keeping its eye on you
Keeping time.
Dancing to the same song.
Not everyone remembers the music.
But I do.
And I can put the needle back on the turntable.

It's not sliding doors
It's not the fork on the road.
It's not a choice
Is it a flashback?
Flash forward
To another time
Or the same space
The lives we lead are like tracks in fallen leaves.
The glitches that appear in your reality,
Are just ripples
No ghosts, no mysterious shadows
It's neither here nor there
Nor is, was.
Death isn't the song's end.
Just punctuation…

TODAY

Today I woke up
Saw the sunshine through the curtains
Today I sat up in my bed
And set my mind to certain
Today I pushed the covers back
And gathered thoughts in my head
Today I put my feet on the floor
And wondered what the day would hold
Today I stood up
I took a step forward
Today I hoped I could be bold
And face my fears
Today I did what I always do
Just get through another day
Today

Today my mind is positive
Thinking good thoughts
Today, if I'm lucky I will survive
Get by, and smile in public
Today my insides will churn
My stomach turn
Today I will try
To do more than get by
Today

Today I may be lucky
To meet no one who will judge
Today my confidence will be strong
Hopefully, all day long
But if it's not
And I have to retrace my steps
And retreat to my safe place
I will try again tomorrow
For tomorrow is another today

NOT DROWNING

I am significant screamed the speck of dust.
To anyone who would listen.
It shouted by the river
Yelled out by the sea
High in the mountains
Even the echo refused to respond.
I have nothing
No thing
One thought goes a long way
Stretching towards
Infinity
It seems
Like a restless, border less
Endless dream.
An echo that continues
Barely audible
Into…
I have nothing
My mind is a blank
A redundant bank
Cashless, Hopeless
Less than zero
Worth less than less
An empty safe
A place of nonexistence
Except…
These words
And with these words,
These very words,
There is proof that I am significant,
Even though, you, you in your high and mighty, supposed haughtiness,
Don't listen.
And if you don't listen,
If you won't listen, Then these words aren't meant for you

YOU THOUGHT YOU KNEW

You told me you were aware of all the dark corners
But I saw you lurking
Skulking in the undergrowth
Thinking that no one knew where you were
But sometimes there are sunny spots for shady people
People who's only purpose, it seems, is to cast shadows
But, stop.
What day is this?
Wednesday you say. "Ah."
It is but just another day.
Another day for hiding away
Escaping those who wish you ill
And yet…
Still!
You make out that all is well
But how deep is that well in which you hide
Inside or outside
It matters not.
You can't recant the clouds
Nor hide in shrouds
Pretend unbowed
Silent or aloud
When friends and friends of friends
Know all is not well
Pray tell,
When did you last reach out ?
No, no. Don't ever be afraid to ask.
If not that person. Then another.
The world isn't full of the selfish and the ignorant
Although, it may seem it is.

Never let the haters get their way
Oh, they will try and have their say
Saying this
Saying that
Making you energetically compromised
Feeling
Beat to death

Death is never far away

But we don't know how
We don't where or when
Or even how
Or...
Even why
Alone or with a friend
One who stuck until the bitter end.
But far is just a concept
As is time
And when your time is up,
When your time has come.
When the reaper reaps
The time for endless sleep
Let it be at least
In peace

So within the time that we have left,
Please stop feeling bereft,
That, is what the bully's want
To taunt you to an early grave
And look them in they eye,
Ignore them and walk on by.
And know that you have friends out there
We are the ones that really care.

SOMETIMES I WRITE ANGRY STUFF

I won't forget
I won't
I can't.
I will still smile
Still be nice to you
It's   not that I don't like you
It's just, well
I won't forget
It's still in here (taps head)
Not in here so much (heart)
I just won't forget
I will still
Applaud you appreciate what you do
But my clapping,
Watch my clapping

It will be still be there
Only just

I do however have the patience of a saint
A little known saint
But still a saint.
Saint Freddie of the fuck you of fools
The intolerance of the selfish, the banishing of the bams.
The saint of those against those who think that only their world matters. And that their decisions only affect themselves.
Saint Freddie;
Protector of those who have been effected by broken promises.
Saint of the spaces left empty by the unreliable not being there.
The patron saint of those who are affected by those who think their problems are the be all and end all.
The patron saint of the people not invited
Not because they aren't liked,
They were just forgotten .
Saint Freddie doesn't forget.
And I won't forget
Unlike you.

LUCKY

We are all lucky,
Even though you don't feel lucky
The fact we are here, alive,
Living in whichever part or this planet we inhabit
Lucky, because our ancestors survived.
Survived wars, plagues , slavery, earthquakes
Storms, illness, and heaven knows what else the past had thrown
As we enter this next year
Another tick in the calendar of life
Hoping against hope that it may be upwards away from the past few years.
Hoping to survive.
Saying in the past
" I will slow down , I will do less."
End up doing more
Role reversal,
Wanting to eat less with more on your plate,
But you can't help to eat words, as you enjoyed what you ate.

And doing so, surviving
Because to lie down means your descendants may not be lucky.
The words we share,
The words we are given to share
Add to the privilege of being still here.
Regardless of how you feel,
The past enabled you to be you today,
And you are part of someone else's past.

SPENDING TIME WITH TOM

It's been a while
Your face doesn't move into the smile for which you are known for.
Your radiant cheeks now take on a sullen look
And when you talk,
Those rare occasions now,
Not like before, when you had all those stories to tell,
When you talk,
The words that come out of your mouth
Are not your words.
They don't sound like your words,
Almost robotic responses
Not even a sadness to them,
Just an emptiness…
Hopeless
A void.
I know that words don't always help,
No consolation in your desolation,
The twists and turns of the truth
You can't brush off, like you did in your youth.
Alone with your black dog,
Walking,
Solitary.
Not talking.

Today
I will see
See who I am who I want to remain
But the mirror is cloudy the cloth nugatory
So I try
To let my true self be espied
It's so very futile

I'm fading away
You can't see me go
You didn't see me stay
Worthless False; Addicted but Trying
Always Going; Still trying
We will see me
Hear me
Patience

I'm not going anywhere
Your silent tears falling on my deaf ears
But I know they are there.
Hiding beneath the surface
Blocking up your ducts
Blocking up your soul.
Keeping you from feeling whole
Keeping you to yourself
Keeping you…
Within.
Without
Without a doubt
Still close to me,
Even though your words remain distant
And slow to enter the world.
I welcome the occasion I hear them.

The knowledge that solitude is not what this is
It brings warmth hope and guilt
The door is opening, the mirror clearing
The tears that are hidden are obvious, it's helping.
The fact There is burden not just for one
No secrets, no rush
A beacon, visibility ,just there, slight, but there.
The journey towards it through the mirror when possible
Not as hard as before , are we all crazy here?
The ink that is drawn in skin once so clear, a pain but a meaning, a clarity of ways
A start, a clock rewound to mark the seconds once more
And an inkling of the voice, smile and flush for this life , it's not over but it's less than it was, I am heard.

I'll walk with you
And talk with you, but only when you need me too.

Thank you. Fin Hall and Janine Rae

DAUGHTER, MOTHER.

UNIQUE

Damaged, broken, struggling?
NO!
Just coping, dealing, muddling?
NO! No!
Weird, strange, odd?
NO! No!…no
Lovely, we applaud?
YES!
Brave, beautiful, soaring?
YES! Yes!
Funny, quirky, not boring?
YES! Yes!…yes.
Positive and free,
I often wish it was me,
Artistic, clever, hard work but deserving?
Yes, yes, yes.
To others it may be slightly unnerving,
A million times yes,
You can keep your critique,
I like unique.

Give me a million dreams and I can show you only some of the best memories

SEEN AND NOT HEARD

No skipping
No jumping
No elephant thumping
No bouncing
No dragging
No beezlebub nonsense

There's this and there's that
It's all that it is
Noise and confusion not required
All just quiet and serene
Pleasantries without carry on
So again we demand insist if you may
No skipping
No jumping
No elephant thumping

LOCKED

In a room with no end pain with no evidence, a muscular ache full and persistent, dull round the edges bleak and morose
Who said it's not real, not worth the energy, the numbness, the sleep with no escape?
A deepness so extreme, so utterly there. Words can't define it or explain the absolute of it all.
Waiting in limbo, a purgatory within life,
for the moment, the second the light turns on.
For the banishment of pointlessness, the return of the beat, slow and regular , the moments that count.
The key to the door.
Then the new day that seems to shorten each time as night arrives earlier, no control and no choice, just there ,an inevitability outwith a simple human's grasp.
The room, locked, again. .

BELIEVE

Do you believe what you want to believe
Do they believe the same as you
Is there belief in breathing, in seeing
Does the belief come from your head or your heart
Do we all believe the same or is it of no consequence
Do we really need to analyse or question
Sitting alone or in a crowd we all believe in something , what and why is between our hearts and our minds .
Neither to condemned or judged by those who are others.
My existence, where it becomes more a desire, a need to nourish the soul.
A change to be made, a goal to be shifted ? A reason to breathe.
To extend my being, my life altered ,chances taken ,a shift if you will,Lessons learned , momentous and held dear.
Done once , an experience to add, a story to tell. My world full to the brim once more, maybe fleeting but never the mundane, never settled.
My impact unknown, but there none the less, a history in my name a version of me, different to all.

I'M FREE

I wish to soar
The sky's are mine
The cloud's my bed
The universe my oyster
But..

QUIET

Hush now, feel your inner senses, pushing to be heard, all at once
A cacophony of non sounding noise, nonsensical literary demands
Breath them in and expel them into the great world, to be let loose in the air
Focus on the quiet, first ..hard to envisage but soon you mellow, your mind listless but healthy, silence the master , defeat the ruckus , inhale the calm.

BLEH

Jelly belly canckles and droopy dog ears
Lines and tinsel marking my years
Pains to stand to walk to climb
This new noise when rising, is it mine?
Glass to see, plastic to hear
Needing to visit after a solitary beer!
Smooth skinned girl stuck inside
Was always so ready for this ride.
Memories made and days lengthy
Filled with so much more than plenty
A good haul with laughs a very good trip
Albeit a lot less time for needing a kip.

INDIVIDUAL

My existence, where it becomes more a desire , a need to nourish the soul.
A change to be made, a goal to be shifted ? A reason to breathe.
To extend my being, my life altered ,chances taken ,a shift if you will,Lessons learned , momentous and held dear.
Done once , an experience to add, a story to tell. My world full to the brim once more, maybe fleeting but never the mundane, never settled.
My impact unknown, but there none the less, a history in my name a version of me, different to all.

SOME

Solitude
Own
Me
Exclusively

POWER

We give them the power that they use to live the lives they wish as we mere ones go without ,having to choose between the most needed of things, do we nourish or do we stay warm?
Our souls are bereft shrivelling in the husks with which we are becoming while they lord over from pillars that we are ungraciously spat on from , the ones we placed them upon.
The lies and deceit flow unbidden and unasked for, washing over to maintain some kind of fake glamour, but some are all seeing and we all live it.
Will they feel empathy as they murder and destroy innocents ? The undeserving, reduced from proud people to meek pleading charities?
Hatred and greed from those that have plenty, they flaunt and deceive from each spew infested orifice , leech and dispose again and again, the lesser of humanities productions, the demons , the crustaceans from which we will never be free.
Can we be? Or will those blinded by the detritus they cast continue to build the pillars higher as if building for deities when in reality they are of such diminutive stature they require us, to believe and not dispute to remain in awe and forgo our basic rights to feed the hunger of the fat political monster!

WHEN YOU SAY

When you say love, you think warmth and butterflies
You think giggles and touching, bedtimes and fever, plans and ambitions not far from each other.
Truth and the lies not always liking, the mundane, the tasks, tantrums and mess, as a pair as a twosome as a team as best.
Looking back as far as the minds eye can stretch , the good and the bad and what each one may forget .
The years as they slip coasting up and then down, in a circle, in an oval around and around.
The care and the ears that are still within reach, this is love , this is warmth and it is what you can't teach.

GRACE

Can we all be granted the grace to just live ,in our own fortitude, with our own voices
There are many reverberating around shouting, whispering all wanting to be heard
It's busy and noisy yet quiet and serene,
Some slow and inverting some at home with it all
It is our power and virtues , our constants and failings
It's humankind, human nature none the same but none different
We all need the grace, the patience and freedom , can we have it?

A MOTHER'S WORLD

Summer heat
Winter sun
Autumn breeze
April showers
All come and pass
Year after year
Day after day
Month after month
Love with no bounds
Unconditional and lasting
From my body to this world
Memories made
Nurturing forever
Through summer heat
And winter sun.

GRAND BABIES

Sweet button nose and tiny pink toes
Smiles and bright eyes that last for miles
Sweet smells and big hugs each time we meet
The joy that you show when it's me that you know
The sounds of your voice like a sweet living song
The emotions so strong and nothing can ever be wrong
The love that consumes nothing can possibly compare
The innocence and beauty like a breath of fresh air.

To be

To be me
Crazy funny erratic
Caring loving in my way
Emotions, too many
Choices , a lot
To be me
Who would want to?

FORGET

Sitting aching high above, missing and drifting. Memories going slowly, ever spiralling . To what was once is no more.

Wrinkles
And grey hair
Age spots and aches
Memories and warmth
To be shared
But with whom
Not you, not now
I tried to , I wanted to
The pain is so deep
The anger so foul
Like fire spreading fast
I can't douse it
I'm trying
The disappointment
And fear
I'm alone
And I'm scared

DID YOU KNOW

You can have an opinion without tearing the world down around, can speak your mind without hurt and disregard.
There are billions in this planet both good and bad, and we all think differently.
Social media, a disease at most when it comes to causing pain.
The lies and falsities again and again, but did you know you can opt to not be part of this.
Keep in touch with old and new, share joy sometimes sad that belongs to you.
There's no need to call out and scar to put fear into others , to be someone you are not behind a keyboard, just a thought; you know…

THROUGH THE EYES

Through the eyes of a child
The world is vast and exciting
Let them be small, excited and noisy
Adults are huge and can be unnerving
Let them be curious and loving
Noises are loud voices can fear
Let them be silent and observant
Houses are full of so many spots to play and be hidden
Let them be mischievous
For soon they will grow, be ripened and learned
And what they had as a child they will pass it on
So let them be, just let them be.

WRETCHED

Wretched beauty in all forms vain and uncompromising.
Withhold the eye of the beholder blinded by virtue.
The one lonely blossom to be left stained, saddened and valued by none.
Honesty disregarded and blasphemed. Wretched beauty in solitude unfolding wings of splendour , hatred and envy.

IT TAKES 2

2 to add more to once what was smaller
2 to find what is finally home
2 to share problems and to support
2 to have love that is forever developing
2 to find strength that alone cannot do
2 is us , it is me and it is you .

DRIVE TO WORK

I drive through the rain muddled roads
Storm whatever battering my car listening to angry hour on the radio, loud incoherent music, a guilty pleasure at times.
Seeing surrounding houses going dark,
Sleep is coming for those but a long shift in the quiet of the night awaits me, mundane tasks, cleaning and restocking while the noise is all around.
The furious volatile weather. Is it pissed off with the world, are we to blame? We name them, these storms? Why? Shouldn't we pay heed as to why
Mother Nature is peeved ,fed up of the chaos and pain we've unleashed? Days too mild for the season, wind too violent rain painful ,things humans have built being destroyed and flattened.
Most others going to dream of what happens in the morning when all this has passed , what damage is left . They will miss it, no second thought given. Contemplation is all I have, as one though what can I do? Is it too late? Is this the beginning of more?

FEATHERS

Floating falling soft and light
Emotions of each unwearable
They were there now they are free
Soaring toward the earth
Like freedom of a gasp
Short and unwavering
Soft and relenting
Are they missed?

WORDS

Where do they come from
My words, my poems?
They rattle around my head
Continuously , never quiet
Always busy always loud
I think in volumes and pictures
So you see my head is full
Permanently , consistently
When I can I put them down
In notes, on paper in verse
This is them as they flow
Some make sense
Some do not
But still they are there
Always, loud in my head.

There is no title here
Just words
Take them as you wish
Is it self entitlement
Is it absurdity
Can we just be what it is
What we are
As it is
As it was
No title
Just words

There is only you and I, nevermore to be anything but what is now and what was then.

Water
Lapping softly against the rocks
History in every soft splash
Knowledge that few will know
Life hidden in every ripple
Beauty untouched ever moving
Calming and today serene.

DAD
Dutifully changing of nappies and wiping of faces
The navy though, always the hankie
Singing unsuitable songs on the bus and in public
The happiness through, always the happiness,
Encouraging and listening, the number one fan
The reassurance though, always the reassurance.
Refusing to age and setting examples of a good life,
The teaching though, always the teaching.

Couldn't ask for a better father to lead me through life.
A legacy though, always a legacy.

Torn

Heart beating in pain
Mind rewinding in constant
The guilt the shame
The could've and should've
A mothers love knows no bounds?
Yet this one is torn, broken, demolished
No longer able to support, keep peace, stay quiet.
One disaster ,one story ,one after another
Never ending, the same but different.
Hatred towards the mother she couldn't be, she struggles with now, the unfixable.
Again the thoughts of how it should be, how the trying wasn't welcomed.
The small child no more visible but still felt and sorely missed
Judging and scornful of only herself, and what she helped mould
Decisions not proper, influenced by too many , torn, left asunder both mother and child
Final nail in the coffin, the door firmly closed, memories bringing tears
How can this be, it was never the plan, the hurting hurt others the cycle goes on
There has to be an end, torn, shredded, destroyed.

HEAL

Heal me she said
As she was blindly led

Save me she cried
As to her face she was lied

Love me she sobbed
As her energy was robbed

What now she implored
As hope walked out the door

I still beat whispered heart
As in its own form of art

You still have me said mind
As only one of its kind

I will be whole she responded
As I will be no more despondent

CONVERSATIONS WITH MY DAUGHTER

It looks like a noose on her neck
Fashion from many moons ago

Suicidal fashion. Love it
Not to everyone's taste

My taste
Bizarre and unorthodox, but is what it is
J rae
A rae

LOVE

Love
Love is a chemical reaction that compels animals to breed,
It hits hard.
Then fades away.

SNOW

Misty air creating crystallised frost
sheets on cold ground,
Sledging down the large steep hill,
Creating a smooth, shiny snow angel,
Skin as pale as snow,
Limbs as numb and frozen as ice,
Slouched in front of a fire place
Crackling like Christmas crackers,
Sipping a warm frothy hot cocoa.

IN THE BLINK OF AN EYE

in the blink of an eye
it's all gone
in the blink of an eye
they don't feel it
in the blink of an eye
they change
in the blink of an eye
it's all gone
in the blink of an eye
it's safe
in the blink of an eye
you're free.
in the blink of an eye
you're gone.
they start to love you.
they start to care.
a single tear drop.
they drop no more.
they're over it.
in the blink of an eye
you're forgotten.

www.ingramcontent.com/pod-product-compliance
Lightning Source LLC
LaVergne TN
LVHW020538160826
845677LV00015B/4132

9798373961592